JAZZ
IN THE CLASSROOM

PRACTICAL SESSIONS IN JAZZ & IMPROVISATION

EDDIE HARVEY

PUPIL'S BOOK

Music origination: Andrew Jones
Illustrations: Shirley Walker
Photographs: page 4, BBC/Bob Komar
pages 6, 14 (inset), 15, Max Jones Files
pages 8, 16, 25, 26, Jak Kilby
page 14, Melody Maker

BOOSEY & HAWKES

Boosey & Hawkes Music Publishers Ltd
www.boosey.com

Jazz

Jazz music began in the early twentieth Century in the Southern States of the USA.

It came about because there were many different kinds of music being played by people whose ancestors came from countries in Europe and Africa, and these different kinds of music became mixed up together. Jazz has changed constantly during its short history and has been called the **Sound of Surprise**.

There are many different kinds of jazz, some of them very old, but people still enjoy playing and listening to them today.

The tape demonstrates four different kinds of jazz. Can you tell the difference between them?

The four styles of jazz demonstrated on the tape are as follows:

- Fusion music or Rock/Jazz using electronic instruments.
- New Orleans jazz, which comes from military band music.
- Mainstream swing of the 1930s.
- Latin/Jazz which is a combination of jazz and the music of South America.

One important feature of jazz is **improvisation**, i.e., making up music as you play it. This can be very enjoyable and **everyone** can have a go. Do you know any other kind of music which includes improvisation?

The Rhythm of Jazz

All rock bands and jazz bands can be divided into two sections: the **front line** who play the melodies and the **rhythm section** who provide the rhythm.

The rhythm section includes the **drum kit** which consists of many different parts, each having their own sound. Here is a diagram of a basic drum kit. As you listen to the tape, see if you can tell which part makes which sound.

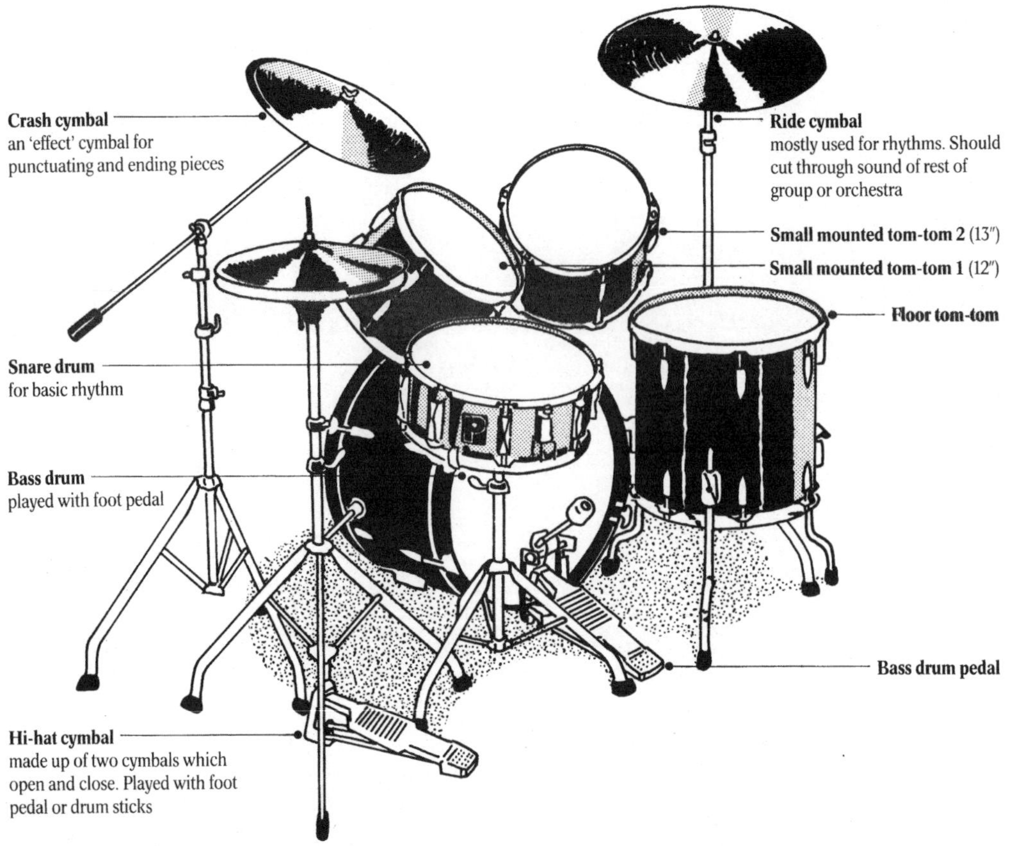

The Body Drum Kit

You can use your body as a drum kit. You can:

- Stamp for the **bass drum**
- Slap our thighs or tap the table for the **tom-toms**
- Clap hands for the **snare drum**
- Hiss for the **cymbals.**

Join in with the tape, repeating the rhythms played by the drums. Start with the bass drum, then move on to the tom-toms, snare drum and cymbals. Make sure that you make the correct sound.

Echo Clapping

Now repeat the rhythms that your teacher plays. This is called **echo clapping**. Take care to stamp, slap, clap and hiss in the right place!

Question and Answer

Structure or shape is just as important in music as it is in painting, sculpture or poetry. In music, both improvised and composed, a common shape is the **Question and Answer**.

For example, how would you answer this question?

Try this one

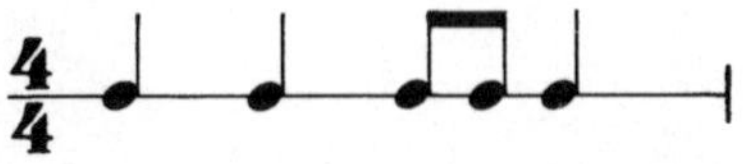

Sing to yourself the tune of *Twinkle, Twinkle Little Star* or *Rudolf the Red Nosed Reindeer* and you will notice that the first statement or phrase sounds like a **question** and is answered by the second phrase which sounds like the **answer**.

Can you think of another tune which has a question phrase followed by an answer?

Practise this question phrase. Remember to leave one bar silent for someone to fill in the answer.

Question (class) Answer (solo)

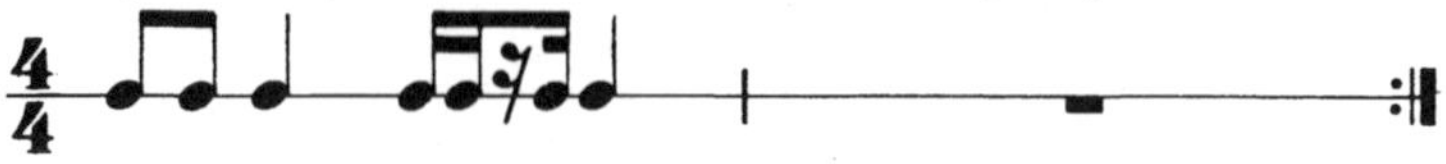

In Session One you made up answer phrases to question phrases clapped by the class. Here is another question phrase to practise. Leave one bar silent for the answer.

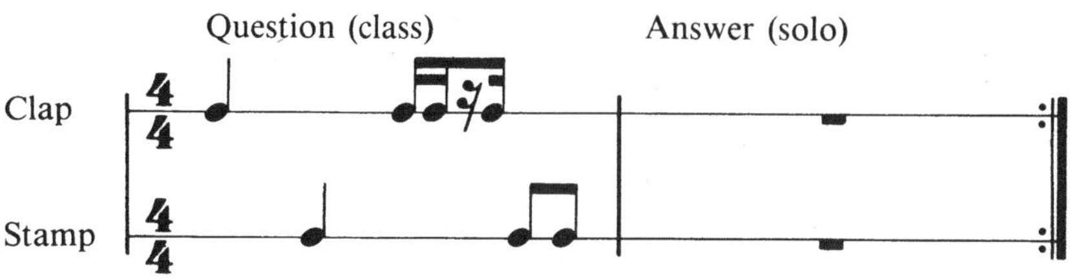

The Class Drum Kit

Rock Rhythm

If you have seen a drummer playing you will know that you must be able to play all the parts of the drum kit at the same time (see picture).

They play the **cymbals** with the **right hand**
the **snare drum** with the **left hand**
the **bass drum** with the **right foot**
the **hi-hat** with the **left foot**

Left-handed players play the other way around.

It takes a lot of practice to be able to do that. You can discover how it feels to be a drummer by pretending that the class is a drum kit. Divide up into the various parts of the drum kit and then play together. If you have instruments, use them, but don't play too loud.

The tom-toms are not included here. They are used in other rhythmic styles, for decoration and in drum solos.

The drummer on the tape will play the rhythm of the bass drum first, then the snare drum and the ride cymbal; finally, the drum **kit** played together. Join in with him as he plays your instrument. Keep the rhythm going while the musicians play.

Swing Rhythm

The **class drum kit** was playing a **rock** rhythm which is used in a lot of modern music.

Another rhythm found in pop music comes from jazz. It is called **swing**.

It swings because the beat is divided into three  instead of the two  in rock rhythm.

Clap this rhythm 

The drummer simplifies this into the rhythm
Try clapping it.

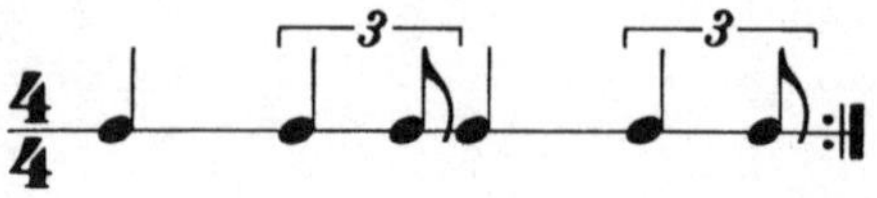

Divide up into the three parts of the drum kit as before, but this time change the rhythm to this:

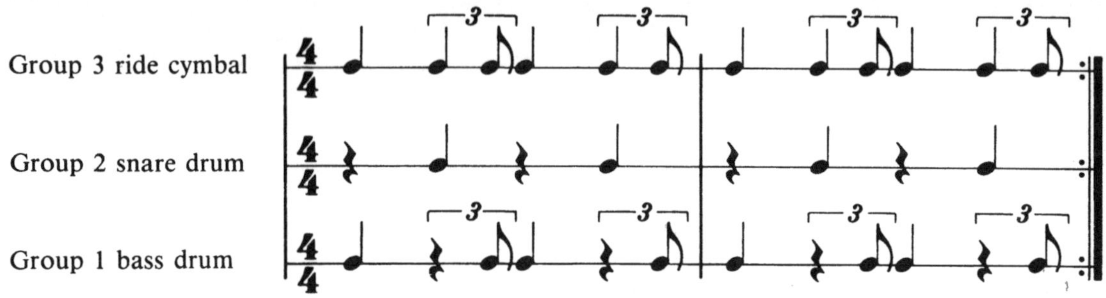

Follow the drummer as you did before. Keep the rhythm going while the musicians play.

Can you hear the difference between the two kinds of rhythm: rock and swing?

Writing swing rhythms using 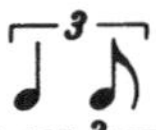 can look rather complicated, so it is often simplified, i.e., written as  but played 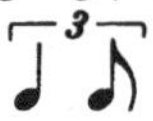

This is shown at the beginning of the music by 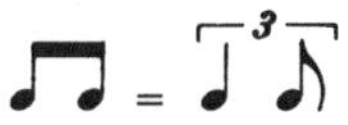

Echo Clapping in Swing Rhythm
Echo the swing rhythms that the teacher claps. Notice how different they sound from the rock rhythms.

Question and Answer in Swing Rhythm
Practice this question phrase in swing rhythm. Leave two bars' rest for the answer.

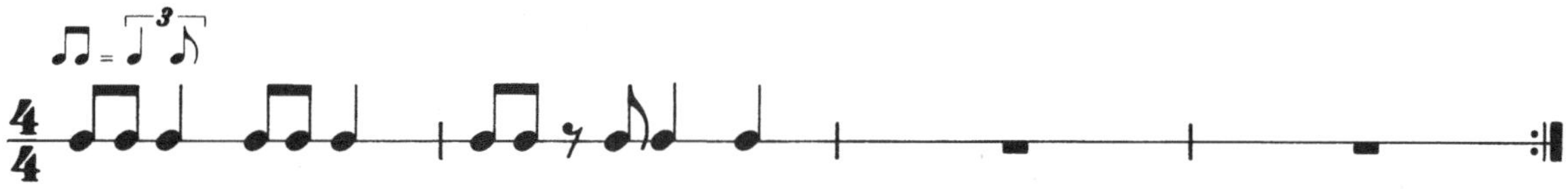

Louis Armstrong, 1960's

Melody Echo Work

If possible, prepare the glockenspiels, xylophones, metallophones etc. by taking off all the notes except G, A and high C.

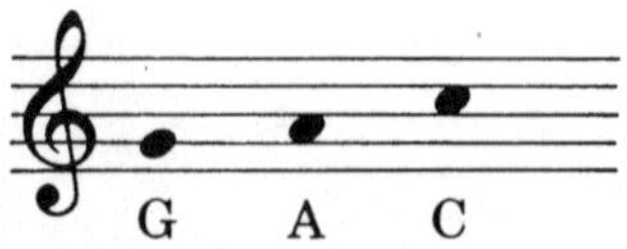

Check your fingering on the recorder/flute/clarinet/trumpet etc. B♭ parts are given on page 29.

Until now, you have only played rhythms.

The teacher will play a note. It may be the highest note or the lowest note, or it may be the one in the middle. Listen carefully and see whether you can tell which note it is, and then when asked, play it!

Now you are going to practise echoing rhythms on each of the three notes in turn. Then try echoing the rhythms on two notes and finally use all three notes. This will give you short melodies which you can use as question or answer phrases.

Question and Answer Work

Practise this question phrase on your instrument. Don't forget to leave two bars' rest for the answer.

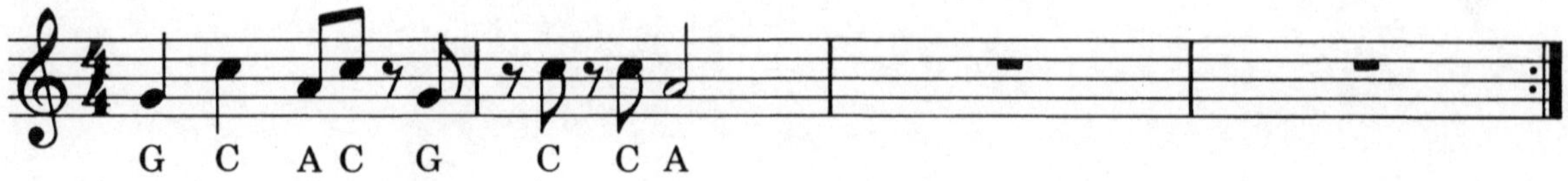

Improvise an answer on one note e.g.

then two notes e.g.

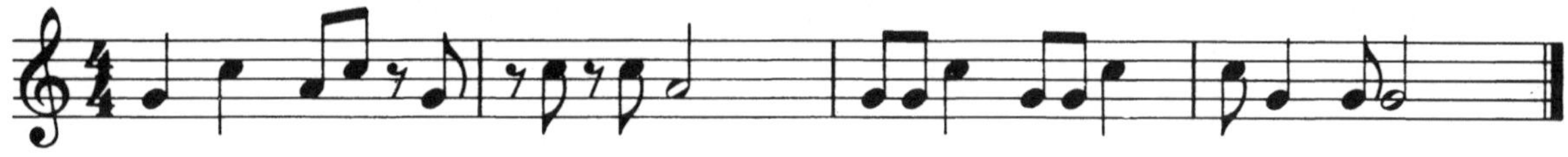

and three notes e.g.

Here is another exercise in question and answer form.
Add the notes D and E to the previous notes G and C. If possible, take off the A.

This exercise is in the old jazz swing style with a two in a bar rhythmic feel.

Wayne Shorter, London, 1985

Question and Answer Warm Up

Using the notes G, A and C as before, practise the question phrase.

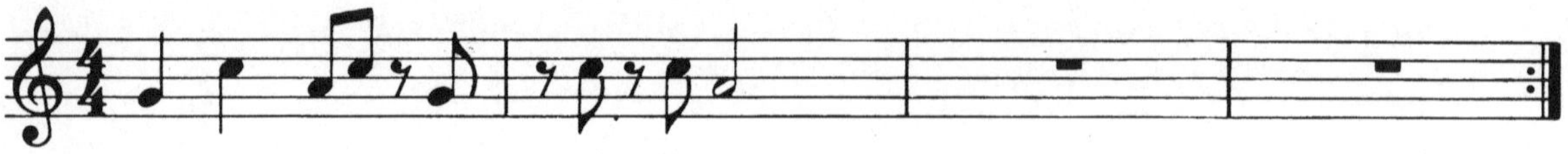

Go round the class playing answers in the rests using all three notes.

The Pentatonic Scale

The **pentatonic** or **five-note scale** has been used to compose music in countries as far apart as China, Hungary, Japan, Scotland, Ireland and parts of Africa. Here is one way of playing it.

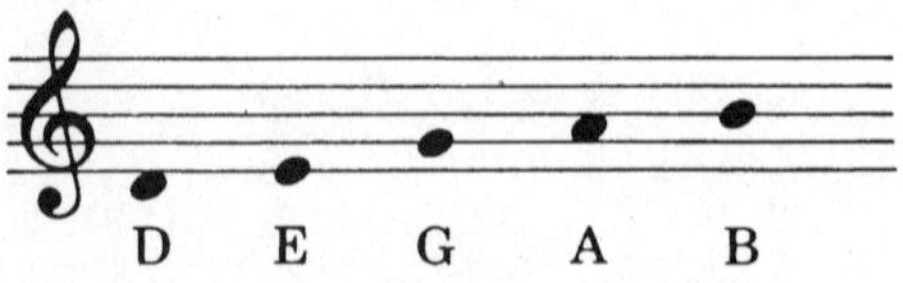

Here is an old Scottish tune which uses the pentatonic scale: *A Hundred Pipers an o'er an o'er* .

You are now going to improvise questions and answers using the pentatonic scale. First of all, divide the scale into two groups; one for the question and the other for the answer.

Here is an example of a question phrase followed by an answer.

After practising these question and answer improvisations learn the piece *Arriba*. The questions and answers are played in the solo section.

Arriba

"Arriba!" is a shout of encouragement which Latin American musicians might use to spur each other on when they play. it means literally, **Arrive!**

D E   G A B

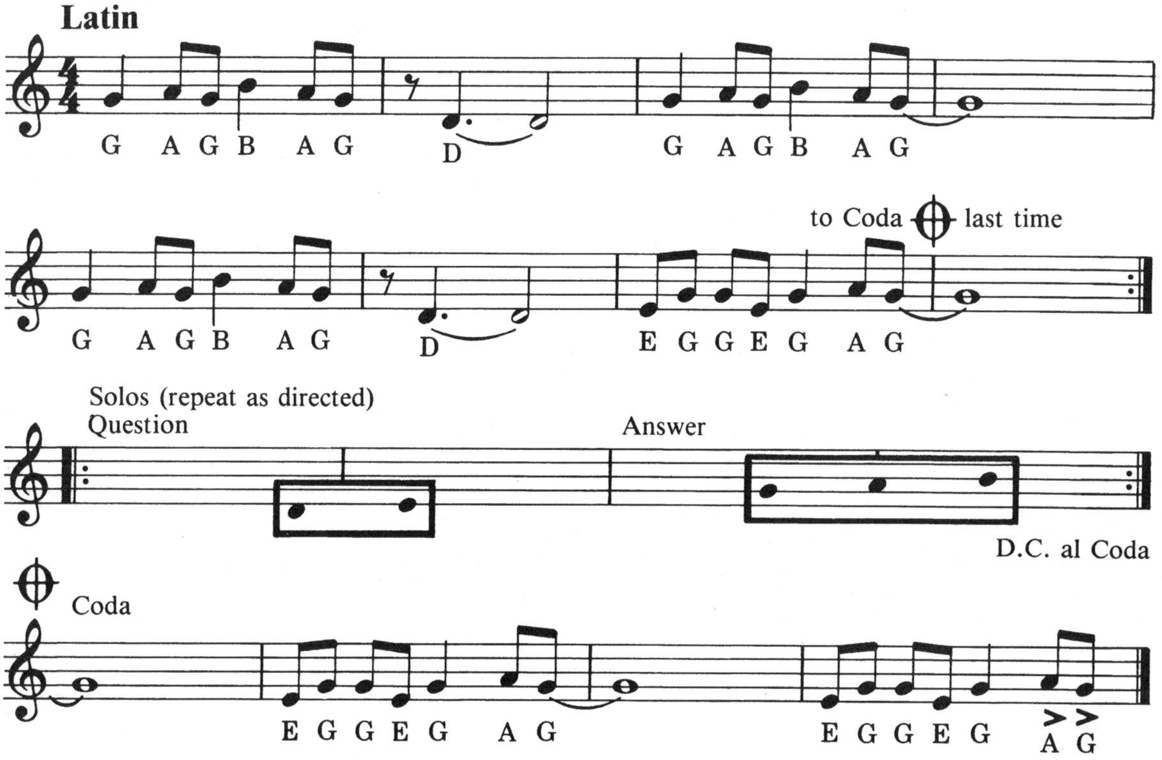

The melody should be learned by heart as soon as possible.

Latin American Instruments

Jazz has combined with the thrilling music of South America many times in its history, with very exciting results. The great feature of Latin American music is its **rhythm**. In order to create this rhythm the musicians use special instruments which are descended from African instruments. You will be familiar with some of them. *Arriba* can be accompanied by Latin American instruments.

The **claves** are played by striking one with the other. The clave that is struck should be held very gently in a cupped hand, so as not to deaden the sound. The hand acts as a sound chamber.

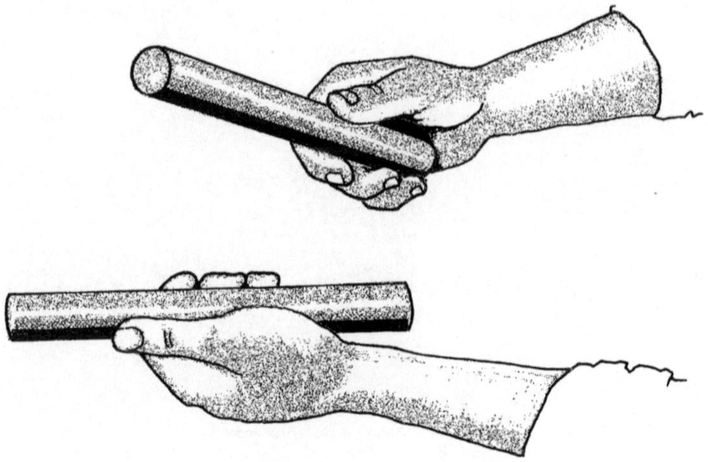

The **tambourine** is held upright and shaken sideways, pivoting at the elbow, not the wrist. The accents are created by tapping gently at the base with the heel of the other hand. For this kind of playing, a rhythm tambourine i.e. without a head (skin), is preferable.

The **chocalho** and the **maracas** are both shakers. Aim to make a short 'click' rather than a 'sloshing' sound. This requires throwing the shot or peas which are inside the instruments, against the side of the container. The action is to and from the body.

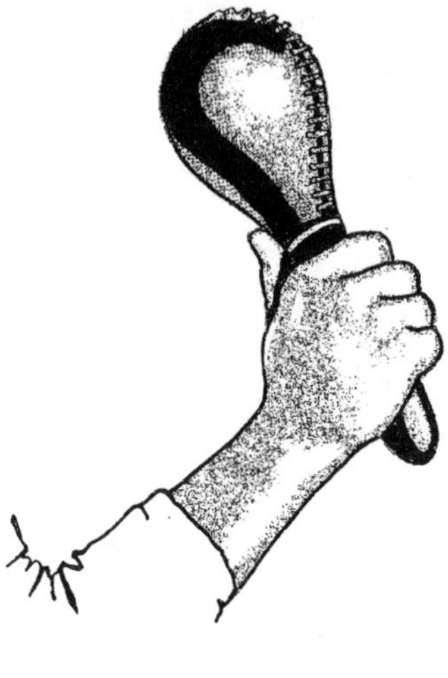

The **triangle** is a familiar instrument in the classroom. In Latin American music it is played damped and undamped. The damped sound is created by holding the triangle firmly with one hand and striking with the beater held in the other. The undamped triangle is suspended loosely on the hand – see pictures. The instrument is played between points A and B (see arrows).

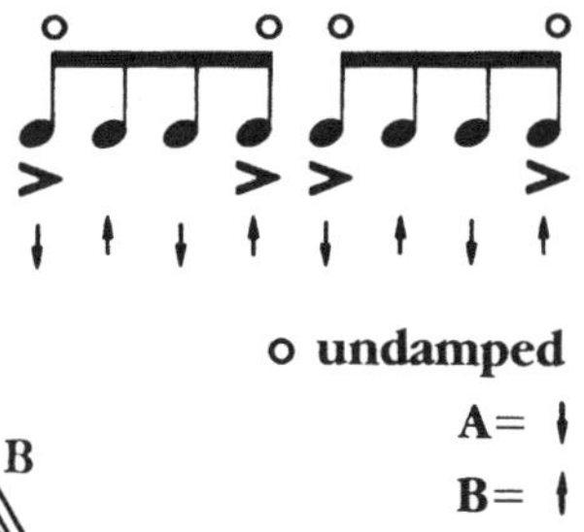

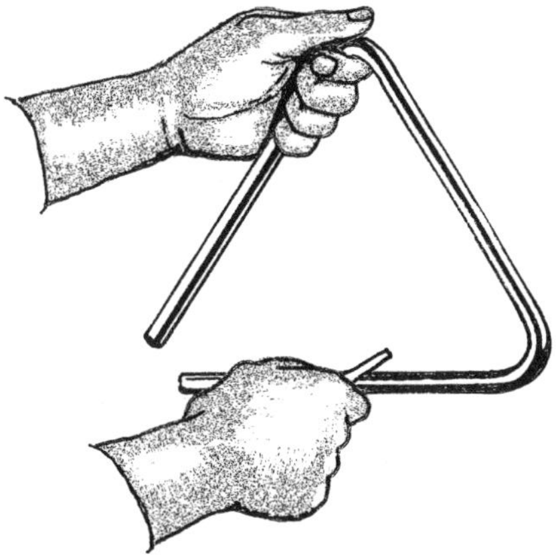

Damped

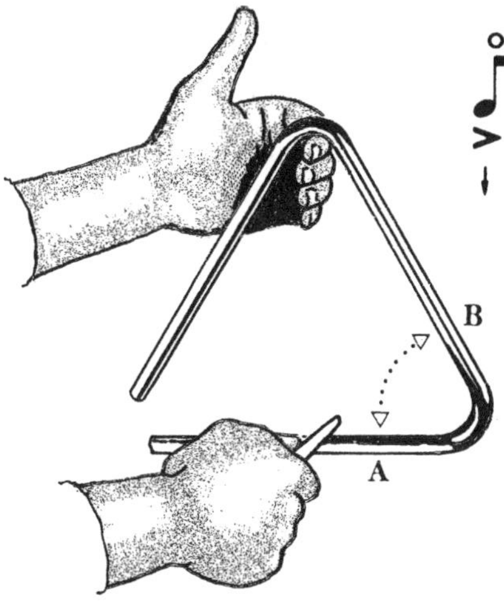

Undamped

The **reco-reco** or **guiro** is a scraper made of wood, usually bamboo. It is held in one hand, pointing away from your body and is scraped with a plastic or metal comb held in the other hand.

Slow

Fast

Scrape in the direction of the arrows.

The **cowbell** is made of metal and played with a drum stick. It is held in the palm of one hand with the index finger at the back. When this finger is touching the cowbell, the sound is damped.

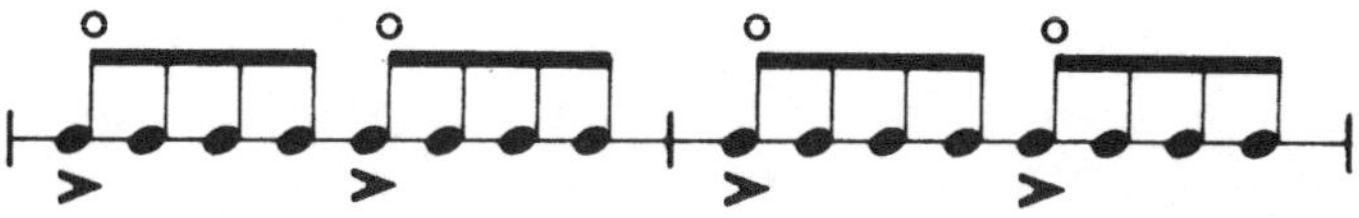

o undamped

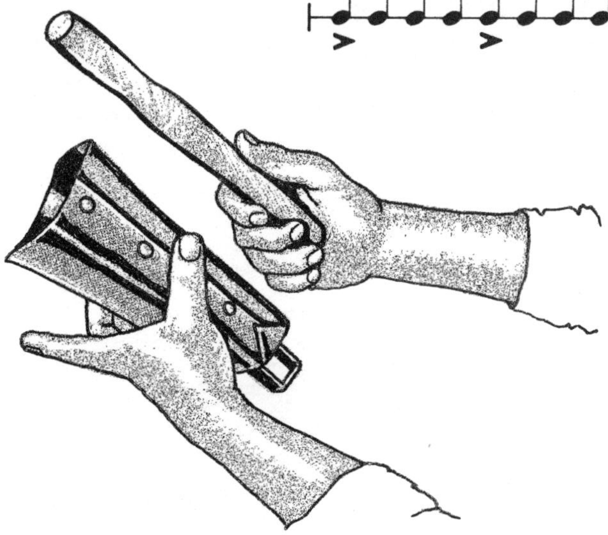

Now play through *Arriba* with an accompaniment of Latin American instruments.

Blues

The **Blues** is a style of music which was important in the development of jazz. It originated from the music of the slaves, who many years ago were transported from Africa to America to work on the Southern plantations. Their music then consisted of songs for working and dancing to and for worship e.g. spirituals. The blues was sometimes sad music but could also be happy. *Boosey's Blues* is meant to be happy.

The piece that you played in Session Four, *Arriba*, was composed using a pentatonic scale. *Boosey's Blues* also uses a pentatonic scale but in a different form. It starts on the note D.

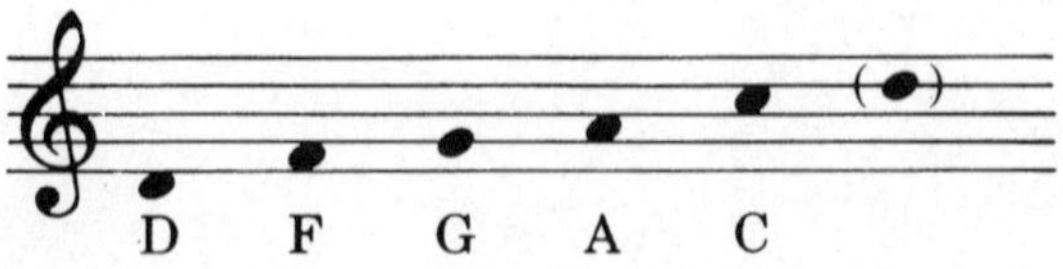

The word 'blue' can mean 'sad'. The reason that the music can sound sad is the use of **blue notes**. In this piece they are the notes F and C. If the note D is repeated, the scale may be divided into two groups of three notes for improvising questions and answers. The melody of *Boosey's Blues* is also made up of these two note groups.

Boosey's Blues

D F G   **A C D**

DUKE
ELLINGTON
AND HIS COTTON CLUB ORCHESTRA
BLACK AND TA
with FREDI WASHINGTON
Hear Ellington Play "Mood Indigo" and "Black and Tan

The Twelve-bar Blues

The melody of *Boosey's Blues* is twelve bars long. The **twelve-bar blues** is a standard form which is used not only in jazz but also in pop music. Famous early pop songs such as Bill Haley's *Rock around the Clock*, Elvis Presley's *Blue Suede Shoes* and The Beatles' *Can't Buy me Love*, are all blues. Is there a blues in the record charts this week?

The twelve bars of the blues are divided up into three phrases or sections of four bars each. The words of the blues are also in this form, using the first four bars to say something, the second four bars to say it again, and the last four bars to finish the statement with a rhyme e.g.

Came to school this morning, dragging my school bag on the ground.
Came to school this morning, dragging my school bag on the ground.
Should've done my homework 'stead of hanging around.

Left: Nat King Cole, jazz pianist and singer; Inset: Duke Ellington Poster, 1929; Right: Billie Holiday, London, c.1954

Modes

The **Modal system** was a very early way of organizing music particularly popular in church music, until the end of the Seventeenth Century.

It was revived again at the beginning of this Century in classical music, and became popular in jazz in the '60s. This was brought about by a famous jazz musician called **Miles Davis**.

The modes still retain their old Greek names and the first one we are going to use is called the **Dorian mode**.

It is easy to find, as it is the scale of C major starting on the note D:

Question and Answer Work

Divide the Dorian mode up into two groups of notes for improvising questions and answers.

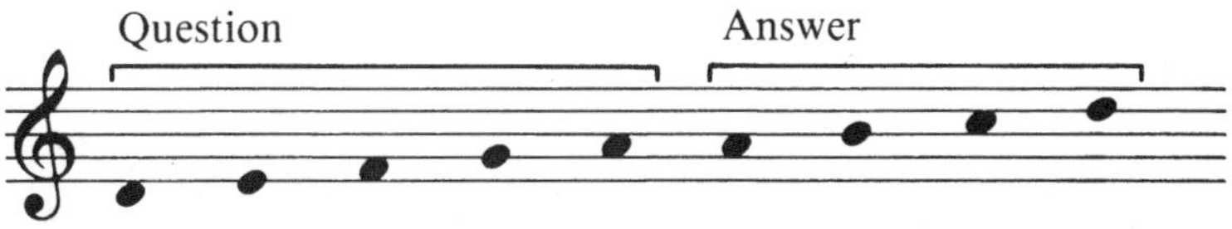

Stanley Clarke (Bass Guitar) and George Duke (Keyboards), London, 1985

Ship without a Rudder

Medium tempo rock

Ostinato accompaniment (repeat as directed)

The instruments of a rock or jazz group may be classified into two sections: the front line and the rhythm section. The **front line** consists of the singers and the 'horns' i.e. saxophones, trumpets, lead guitar, trombones or strings. The **rhythm section** includes the rhythm guitar, piano or keyboards, double bass or bass guitar, percussion and drums. To perform *That Dusty Ol' Road* you will need a front line and a rhythm section.

Some modes have a sad or **minor** sound; others have a bright, **major** sound. The Dorian mode used in *Ship without a Rudder* had the minor sound. You are now going to play a piece in a mode that has a bright, major sound. This is the **Myxolydian mode** and it consists of the following notes:

Divide the mode up into two groups of notes for improvising questions and answers.

That Dusty Ol' Road

Medium tempo swing

B Optional second theme

Rhythm Section

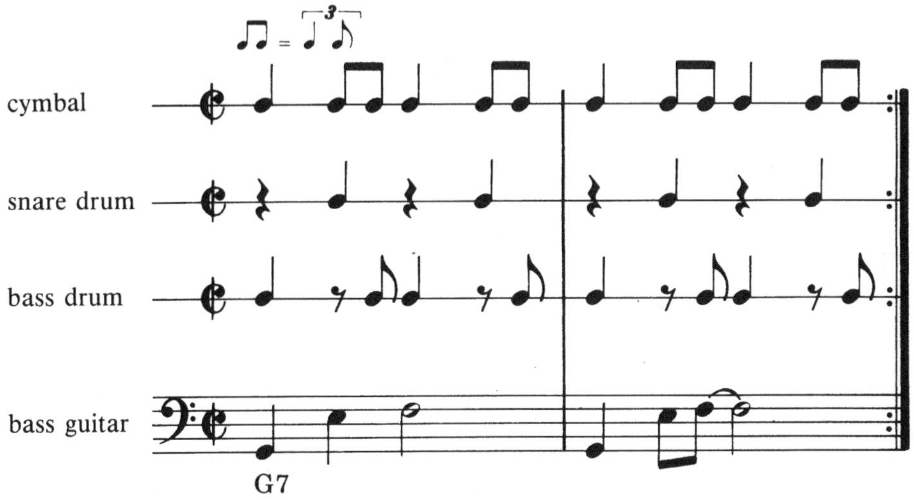

$\frac{3}{4}$ *time*

So far in this book, we have played music in $\frac{4}{4}$ or 𝄵 time. These have four or two beats in the bar.

Rock and jazz music are also played in other times such as $\frac{2}{4}$, $\frac{3}{4}$, $\frac{5}{4}$ and even $\frac{7}{4}$
Try clapping these rhythms. Repeat ad. lib.

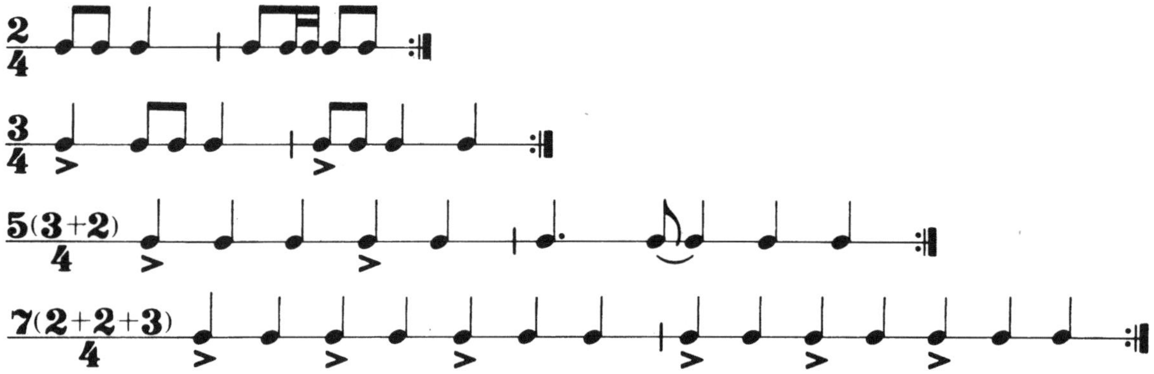

Now the class drum kit can play in $\frac{3}{4}$ time, a **jazz waltz**.

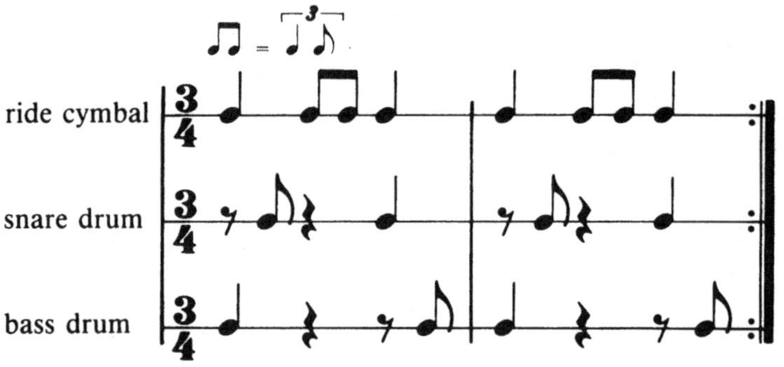

Follow the drummer on the tape as before. Keep the rhythm going while the musicians play.

The piece in this session is called *Waltz of the Pyramids*. It is in $\frac{3}{4}$ time and uses the Phrygian mode. This is a minor-sounding mode beginning on E.

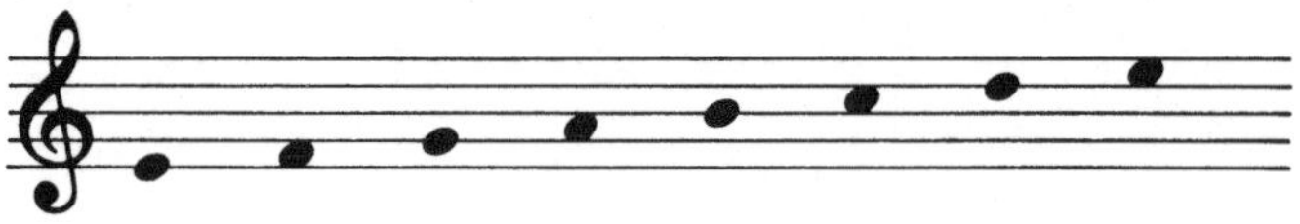

Divide the mode up into two note groups as before.

Waltz of the Pyramids

Fast jazz waltz

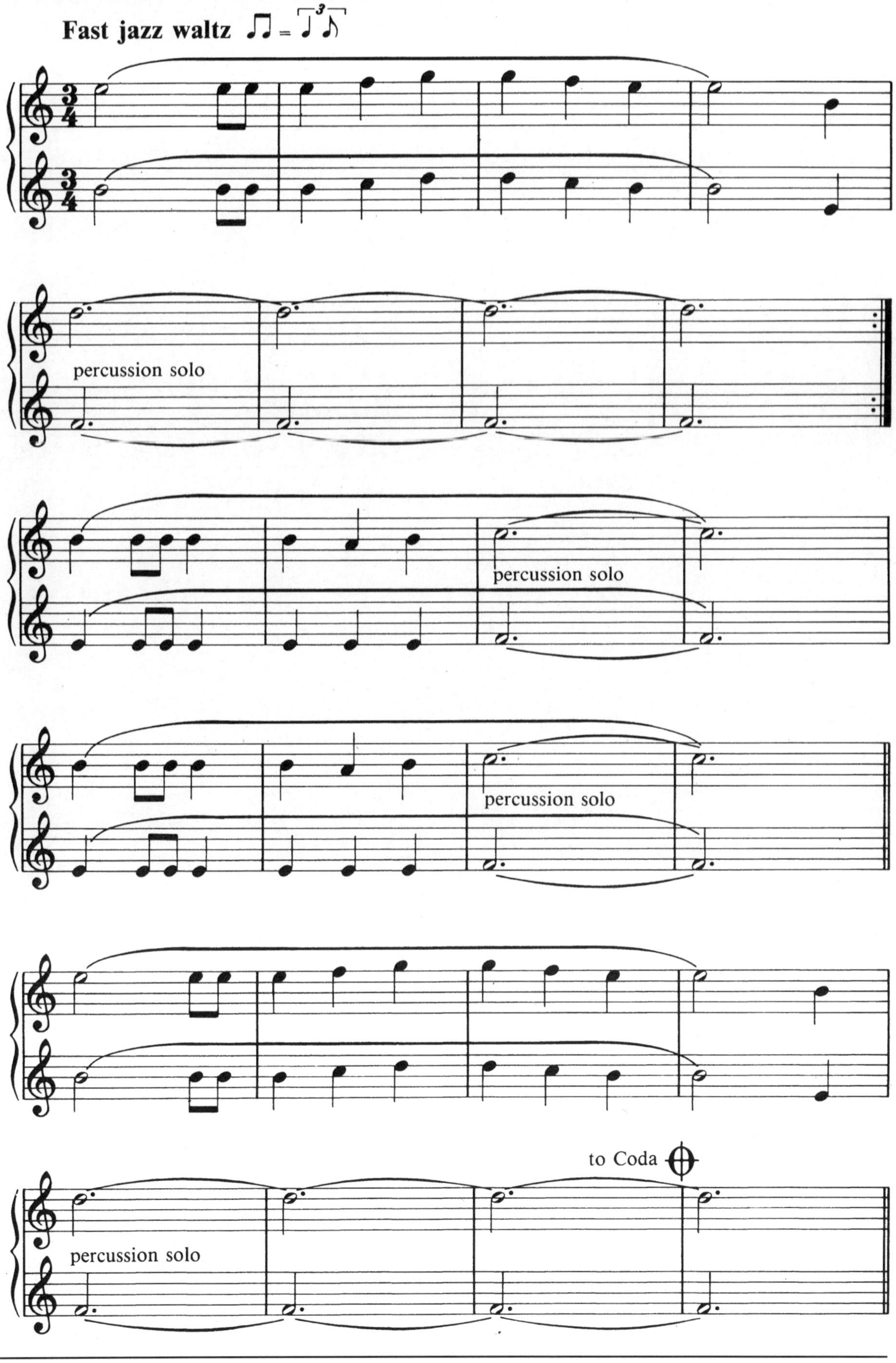

Solos (repeat as directed)
Question

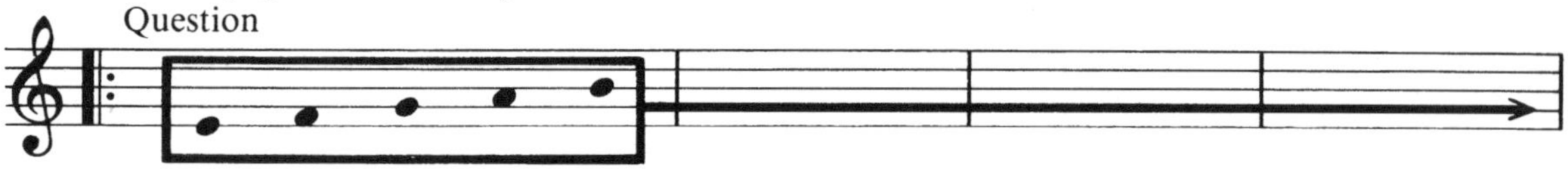

Answer

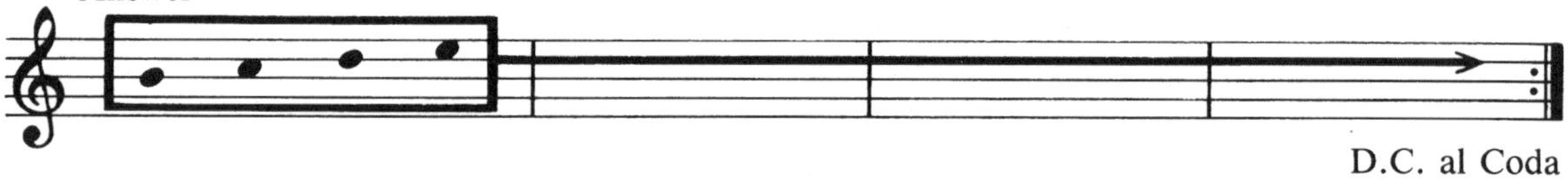

Coda

Bass ostinato

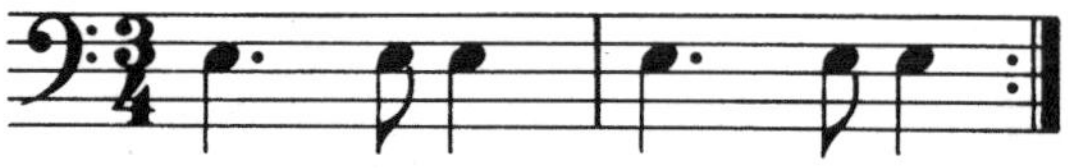

Optional ostinato accompaniment to solos
(repeat as directed)

Rhythm Section

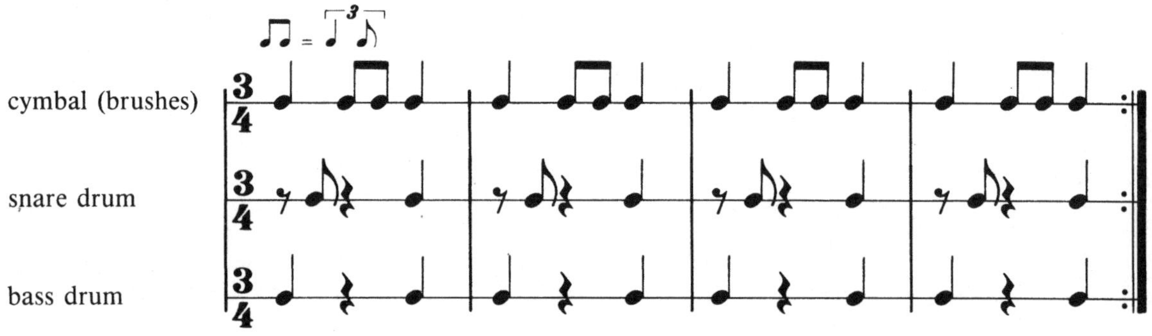

Harmony

When you play tunes or melodies you play single notes one after the other.

When you play two or more notes at the same time, it is called **harmony**.

To do this, you have to choose the **intervals** between notes very carefully because all intervals sound different.

Play or listen to these intervals. Which ones do you prefer?

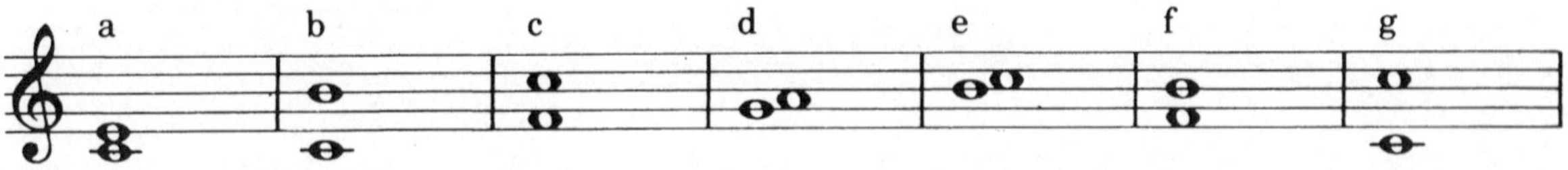

In modern harmony these intervals are mixed up together to make exciting-sounding chords. Listen to these!

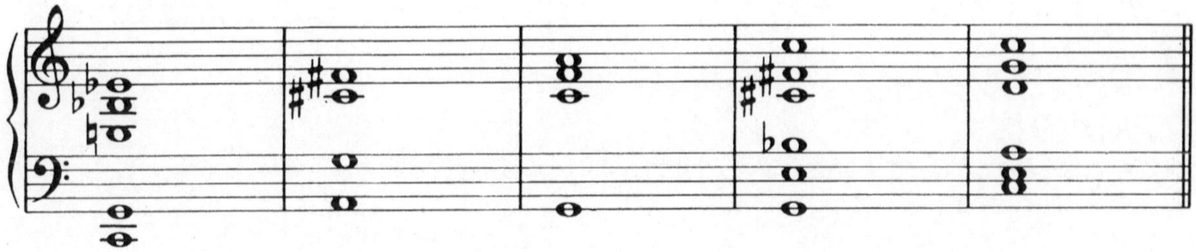

But first you must learn about simple chords.

The simplest chords are called **triads** because they consist of three notes.

In a triad, the notes are spaced at the interval of a third e.g. C, E and G make a triad, so do D, F and A. Play these triads.

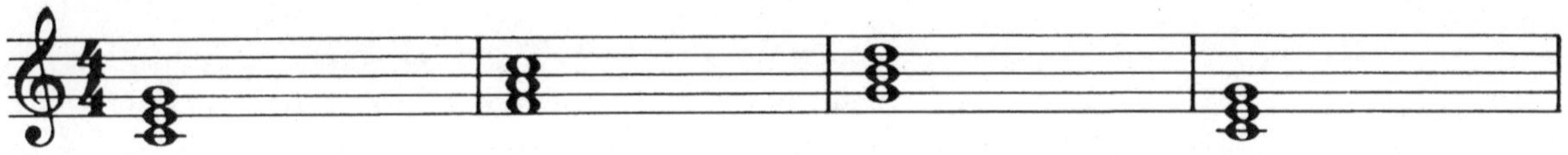

Played one after the other, these notes can make a tune.

Longer tunes are made up of bits of scales, and bits of **chord tunes**. Remember this when you are improvising or making up tunes.

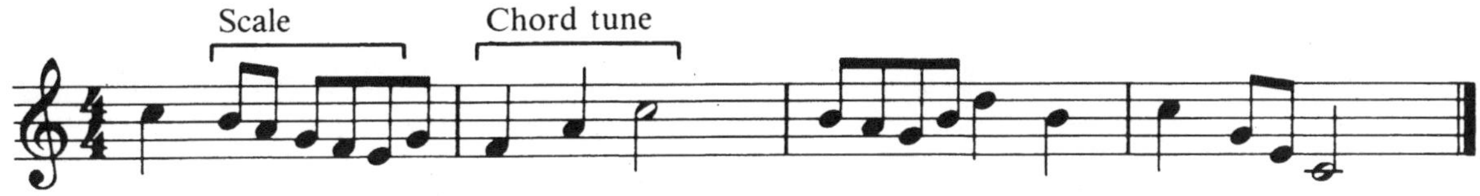

Make up answers to these chord tunes.

1 Question (class) Answer (solo)

2

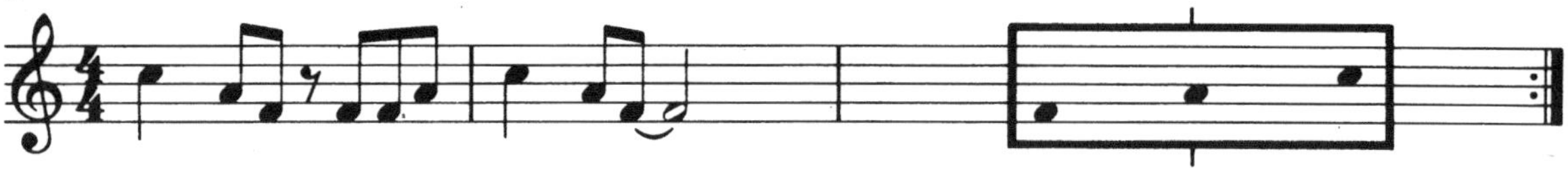

3

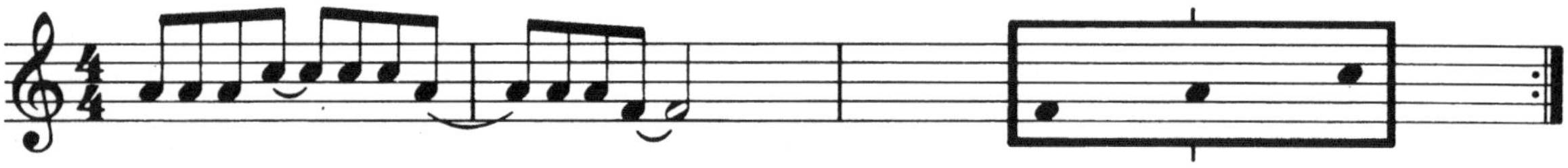

Naming Chords

Chords can be named in three ways. Firstly, they can be called after the **root** note i.e. the lowest note of the chord. Secondly, they can be called after the type of chord i.e. major or minor. Thirdly, they can be described after the degree of the scale on which they are based.

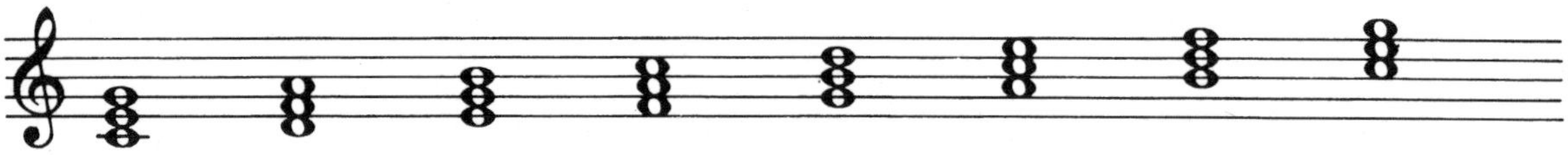

I II III IV V VI VII

C major F major G major

I, IV, V, I Calypso is a tune constructed of chord notes. A **calypso** is a song originally from Trinidad. The words are usually topical and often made up 'on the spot'. It has a catchy  rhythm. Rehearse the melody first and then improvise solos using the same notes.

I, IV, V, I Calypso

Solos (repeat as directed)

This tune may be accompanied by classroom instruments, playing chords on the first beat of each bar, and by unpitched Latin American instruments e.g. chocalho, guiro and claves.

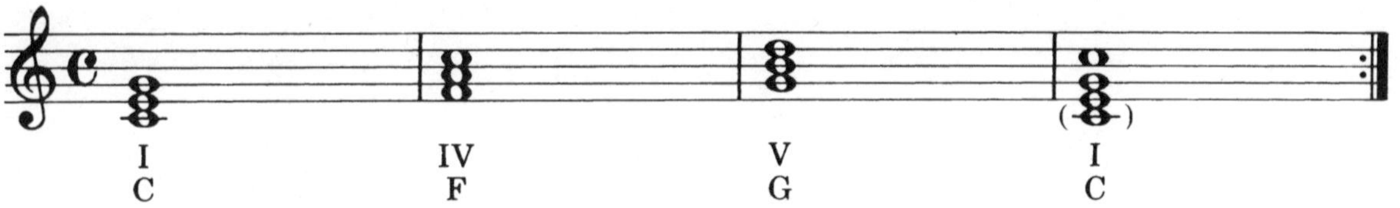

Now try improvising a solo using scales built on each chord.
● = chord notes ○ = passing notes

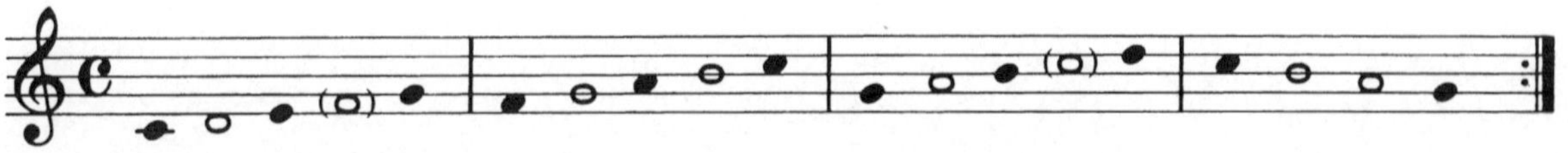

Wynton Marsalis (Trumpet) and Bill Pierce (Tenor Sax) with Art Blakey's Jazz Messengers, 1981

Triads can be constructed on every degree of the major scale. Some of the chords are major and some are minor. You have played the major chords I, IV and V in Session Nine. Now you can play chords II and VI which are minor.

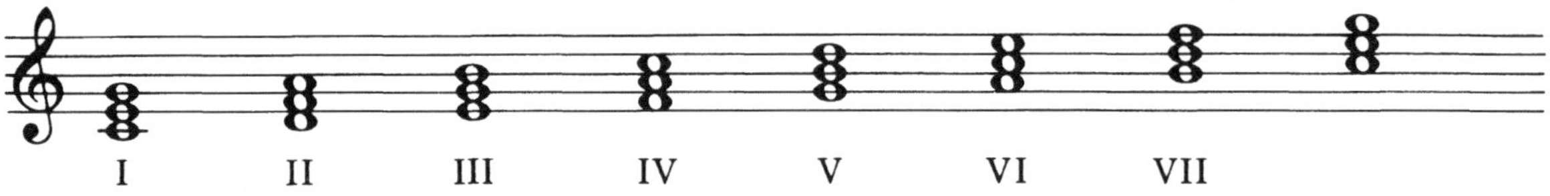

II, V, I, VI Reggae is another tune constructed of chord notes. As before the tune may be accompanied by instruments playing chords on the first beat of each bar.

II, V, I, VI Reggae

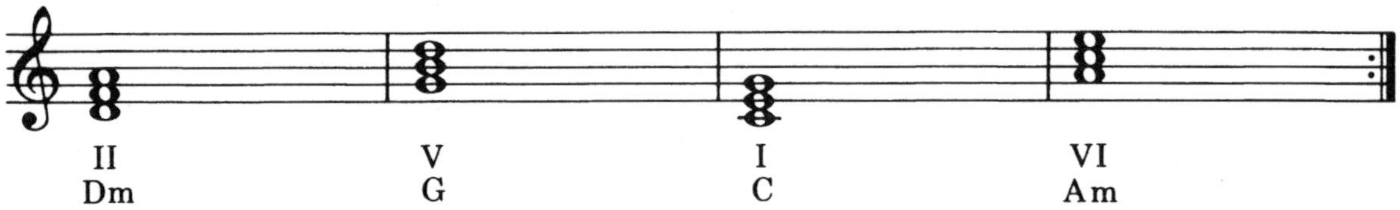

Summer Song uses the same chord sequence i.e. II, V, I, VI.

Pat Metheny, 1978

Summer Song

Swing
A
mf
Dm7 G7 C6 Am7 Dm7 G7 C6 Am7
Dm7 G7 C6 Am7 Dm7 G7 C6
B
1
2
cresc. (2nd time only)
G7 Dm7 G7 Dm7
C
Dm7 G7 C6 Am7 Dm7 G7 C6 Am7
Fine
Dm7 G7 C6 Am7 Dm7 G7 C6

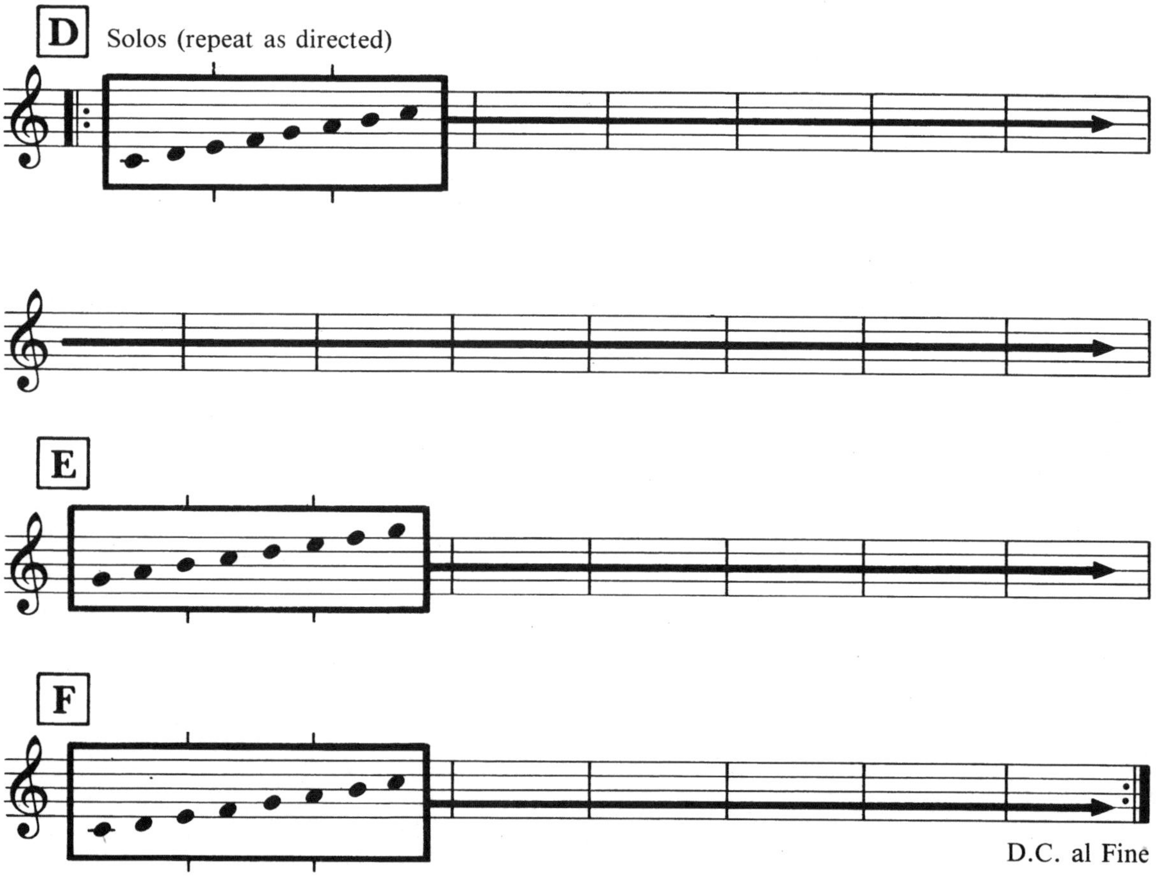
D
Solos (repeat as directed)
E
F
D.C. al Fine

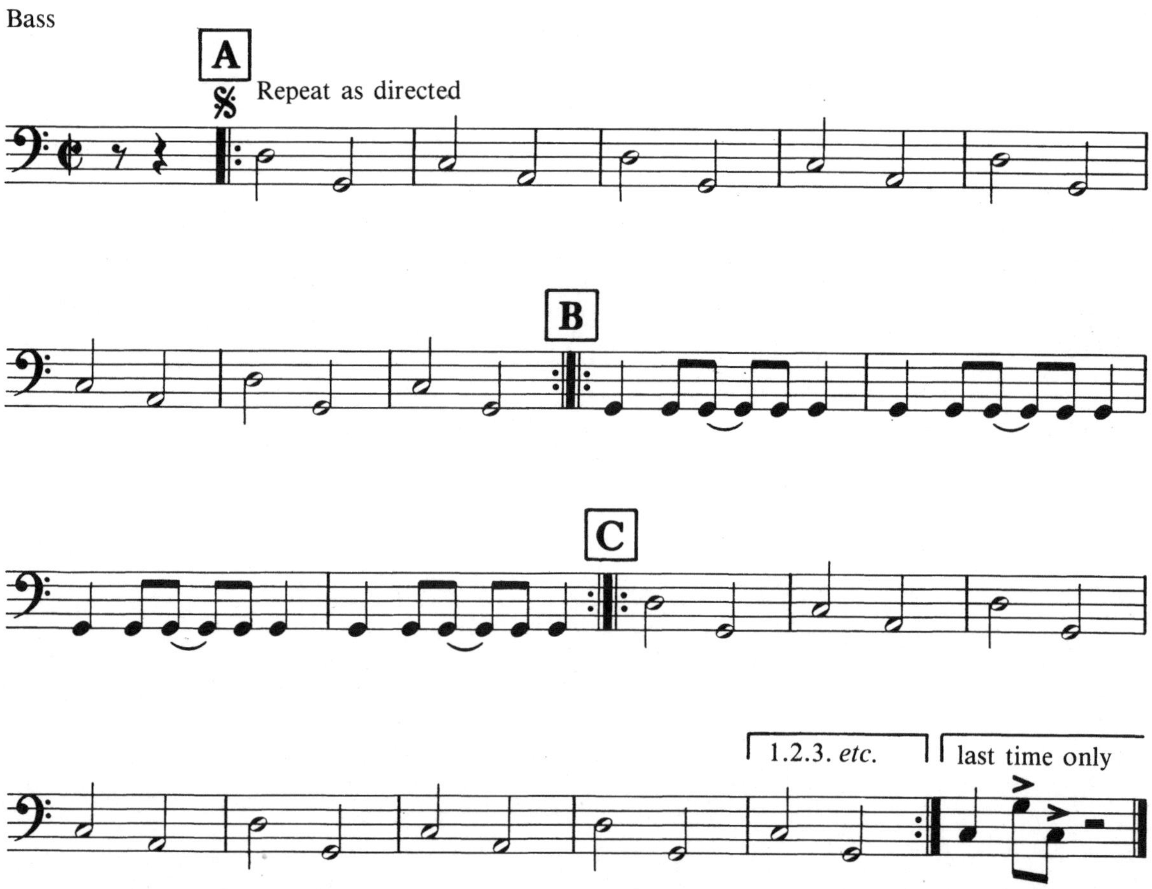
Bass
A
Repeat as directed
B
C
1.2.3. etc.
last time only

B♭ section
Session Three

page 7

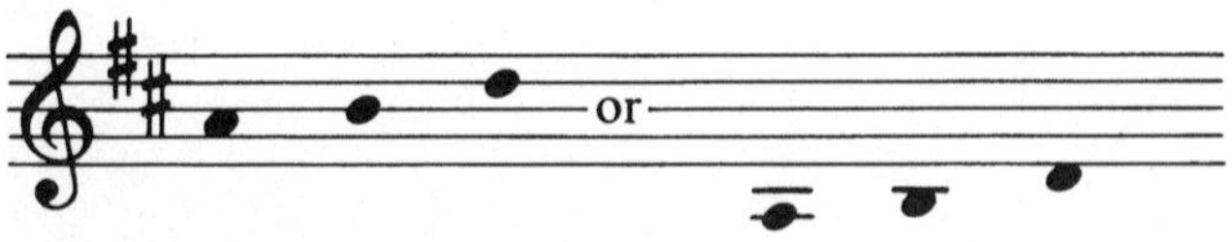

page 7

Improvise an answer on one note e.g.

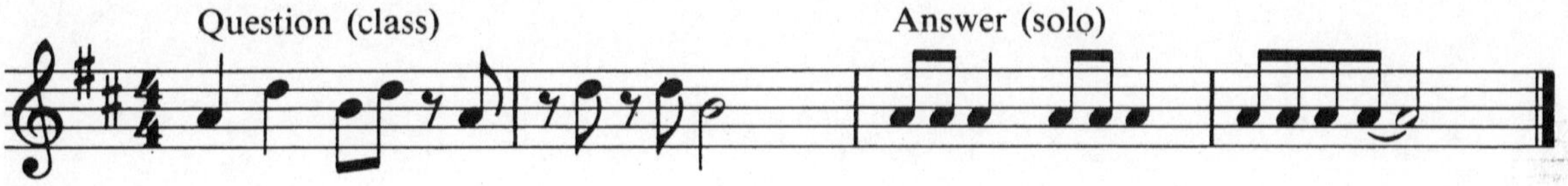

then two notes e.g.

then three notes e.g.

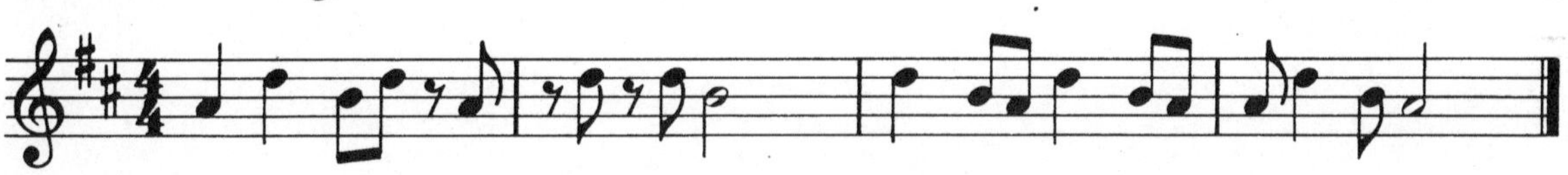

page 8

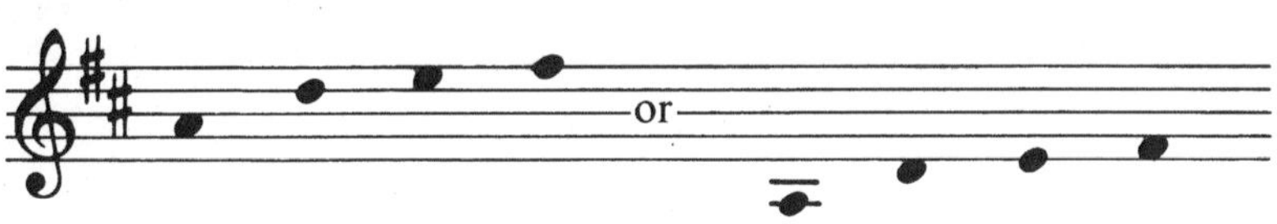

or

Session Four

Arriba

page 10

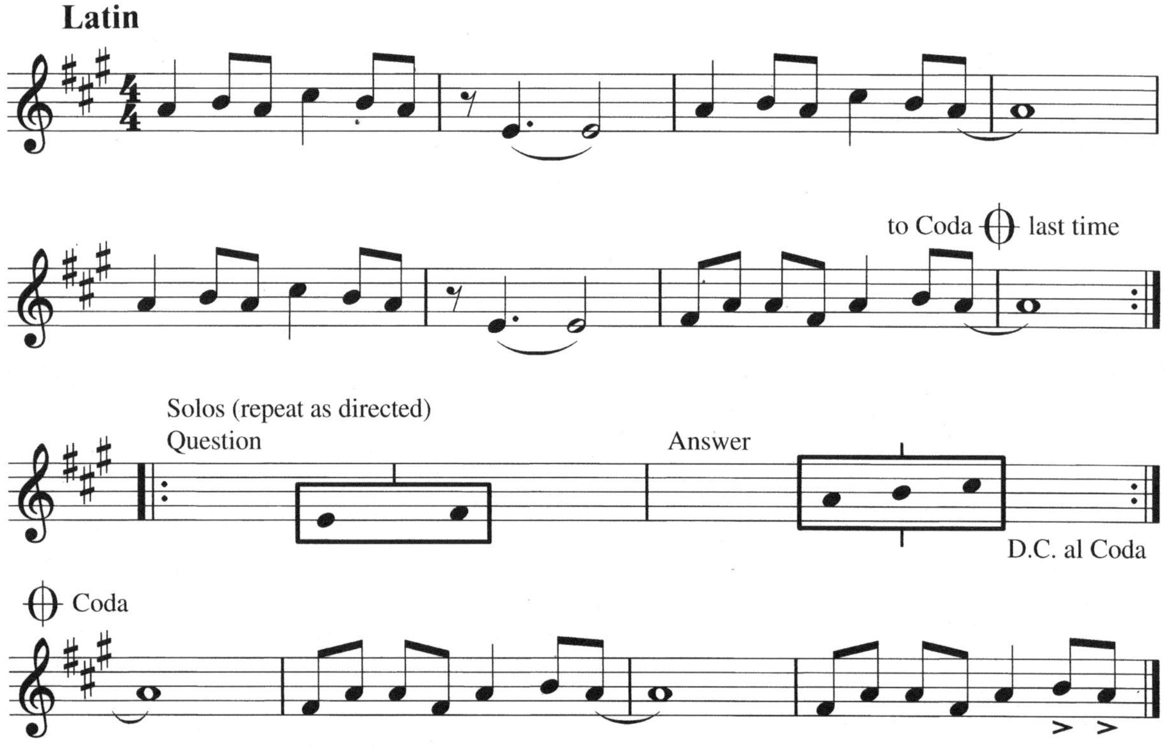

Session Five

Boosey's Blues

page 13

Session Six

page 17

Ship without a Rudder

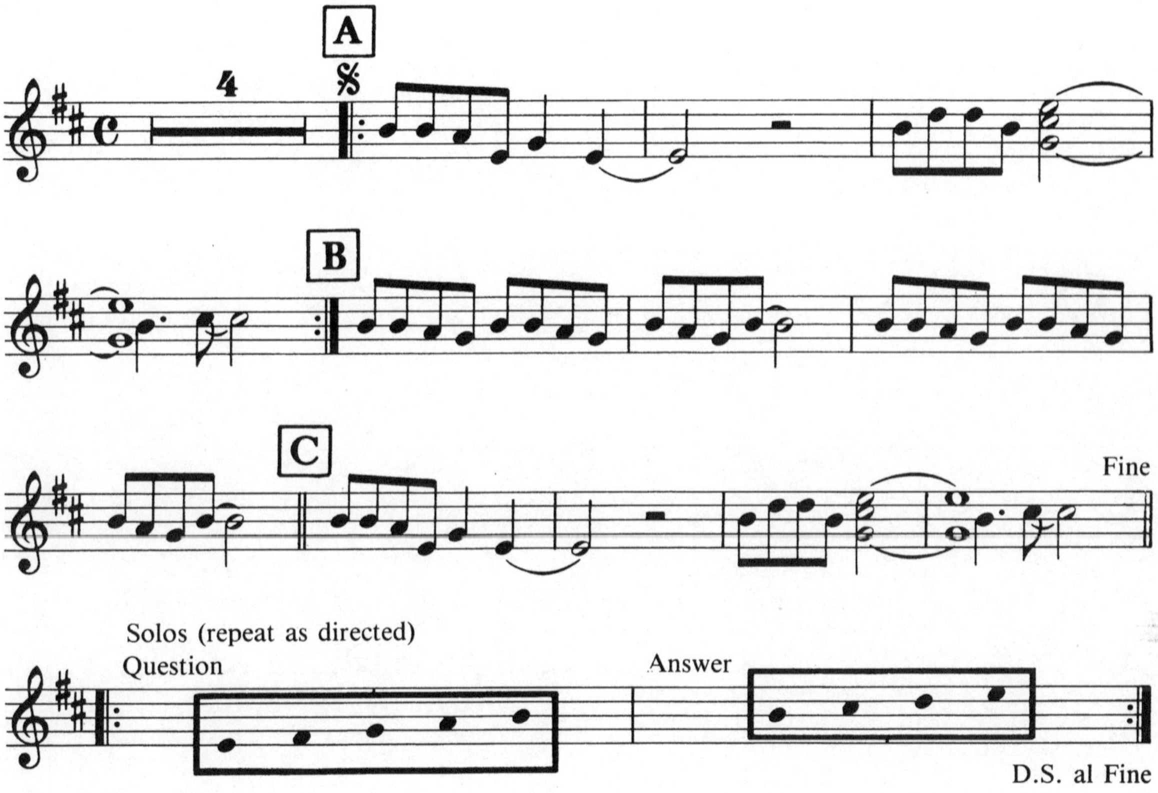

Session Seven

page 18

That Dusty Ol' Road

Medium tempo swing

B
Optional second theme
mf
C
Fine
Solos (repeat as directed)
Question
Answer
D.S. al Fine

page 21

Waltz of the Pyramids

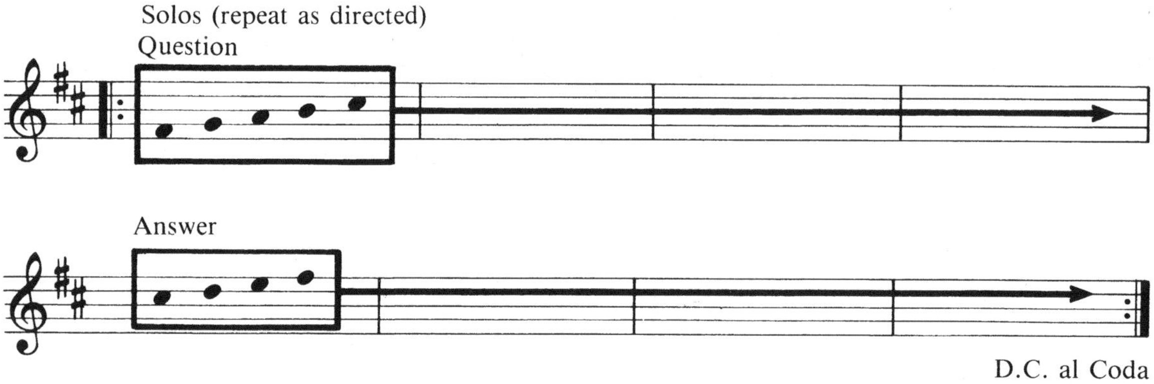

Session Nine

page 24

page 24

I, IV, V, I Calypso

Solos (repeat as directed)

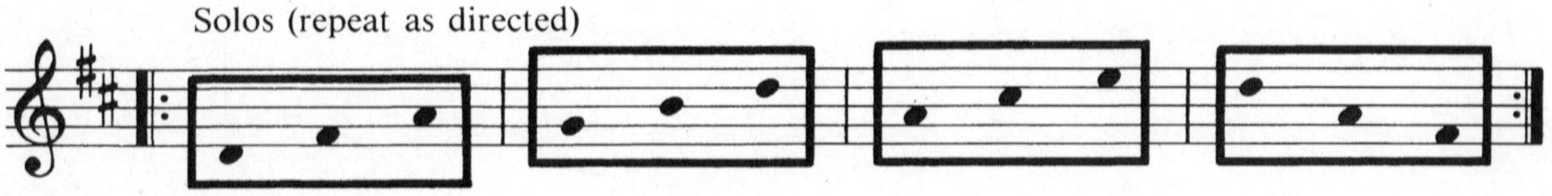

or

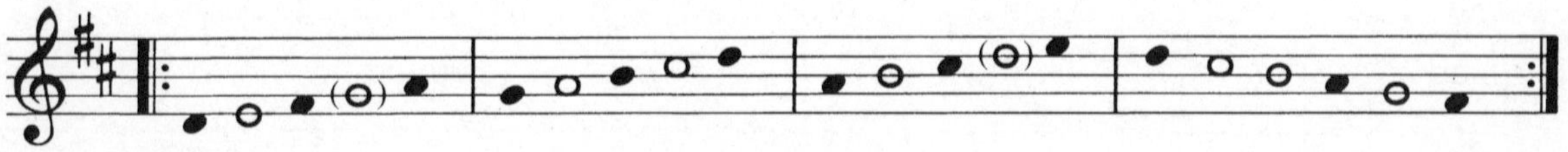

Session Ten

page 26

II, V, I, VI Reggae

Solos (repeat as directed)

page 27

Summer Song